Anonymous

The Metropolis Explained and Illustrated in Familiar Form

Vol. 1

Anonymous

The Metropolis Explained and Illustrated in Familiar Form
Vol. 1

ISBN/EAN: 9783337292393

Printed in Europe, USA, Canada, Australia, Japan

Cover: Foto ©Thomas Meinert / pixelio.de

More available books at **www.hansebooks.com**

THE METROPOLIS EXPLAINED AND ILLUSTRATED.

STAIRS FROM CARRIAGE ROAD TO TERRACE, CENTRAL PARK.

THE METROPOLIS

EXPLAINED AND ILLUSTRATED

IN FAMILIAR FORM,

WITH A MAP.

NEW YORK:
PUBLISHED BY DEVLIN AND COMPANY.
1871.

TO NEWSPAPER EDITORS AND PUBLISHERS.

We hope that this little work may arrest the attention of newspaper editors sufficiently to induce an examination, and that the intrinsic usefulness of the book, which cannot fail to be very great to all visitors not familiar with New York, will induce the announcement that we will be happy to present a copy to any one applying for it by mail or in person at either of our stores.

We are also publishing separately in neat form, the portion of this book devoted to the Central Park, for distribution in the same manner.

DEVLIN & CO,

Box No. 2256, P. O.

BROADWAY, Cor. GRAND STREET.

BROADWAY, Cor. WARREN STREET.

NEW YORK, *March,* 1871.

RIVERSIDE, CAMBRIDGE:

ELECTROTYPED AND PRINTED BY

H. O. HOUGHTON AND COMPANY.

NOTE.

FEELING that there existed a great want, on the part of strangers visiting New York City, of some simple, practical, and convenient book that would explain the locality and means of access to the leading points of interest in the metropolis, and more especially to the Central Park, we have caused this little volume to be prepared. We send it forth upon its mission, in the hope that it may prove helpful and useful to the stranger within our gates.

DEVLIN & CO.

INDEX.

THE CENTRAL PARK.

It is not within the scope of this article to attempt an exhaustive treatise upon the Central Park, either as a whole or in any of its many interesting phases. That has been done so ably, not only in the comprehensive reports of the commissioners, but also in the beautiful work upon the subject published by Messrs. F. J. Huntington & Co., — from which authorities we have drawn largely for the basis of this article, — that to presume to add anything thereto, within these narrow limits, would be an absurdity. Our purpose simply is, to give such facts, descriptions, and directions, in familiar form, as will assist the stranger in seeking for and appreciating the beauties of the Park; to help the enjoyment by desirable information, and useful suggestion, and not to hinder it by presenting anything beyond that which is essential to an intelligent understanding of its history, plan, and leading features.

HOW TO GO TO THE PARK.

The public conveyances that lead to the immediate vicinity of the Park, are the street cars, as follows, namely : —

Second Avenue Railroad, from Peck Slip.

Third Avenue Railroad, from the lower end of the Park opposite the Astor House.

Eighth Avenue Railroad, from both Vesey and Canal streets, and Broadway.

The cars of the above roads all run beyond the upper end of the Park, thus affording an opportunity to enter by the gates on 59th Street, or at either of the upper entrances.

Sixth Avenue Railroad, from both Vesey and Canal streets, and Broadway.

Seventh Avenue Railroad, from both Barclay and Broome streets, and Broadway.

Central Park, North and East River Railroad (Belt).

Eastern Division, from South Ferry by a circuitous route through the east side of the city to the Park.

Western Division, from South Ferry *via* river front and Tenth Avenue to the Park.

The cars of these last-named roads do not go beyond 59th

Street, thus necessitating an entrance to the Park by some of the gates at the south end.

Fourth Avenue Railroad, from the lower end of the Park opposite the Astor House, *via* the Bowery, Fourth Avenue, and Madison Avenue, to 89th Street. This road runs one block east of the Park, from 59th to 86th streets.

There are also several omnibus lines that run within a few blocks of the Park.

ORIGIN AND EARLY HISTORY.

It was about the year 1830 that the city of New York started from the quiet and steady progress that thus far had been its characteristic, and, with a suddenness almost startling, took the place which she still holds, and will continue to maintain, as the Metropolis of the Western Hemisphere.

This change came so quickly that in a short time the entire elements of the city underwent a change. Business grew rapidly, population came pouring in from all sides, building increased, and business interests began that demand upon the premises used for residences that is still unsatisfied. This change soon deprived the city of the quiet gardens and detached dwellings that afforded an opportunity for pure air; their places being filled by solid blocks of houses and stores that increased the evil then plainly appearing, namely, the want of breathing space.

As the city grew in population, it became a constantly more settled fact, that for the majority of the people, especially for those of limited means, escape from the city for a little rest or recreation was almost an impossibility. The localities accessible by water were too remote, or not reputable; and to the north of the city there was only a barren waste, save for those whose means and leisure afforded a private equipage wherewith to enjoy the drives on Harlem Lane, and the Bloomingdale Road.

These facts developed in the public mind a longing for a place where blue sky and fresh air, grass, trees, and flowers, might be enjoyed with little loss of time, or expenditure of money. It was about the year 1848 that the patient and long-suffering people of New York began to find that something must be done to supply this daily growing want. There was no place within the city limits in which it was pleasant to walk or ride; no water on which it was safe to row, no play-ground for children, no spot for the weary to rest body or brain in the contemplation of the beauties of nature.

It was during this year that Mr. A. J. Downing first gave public expression, through the columns of the "Horticulturist," to this universal want of a great public park. In 1850 he made a voyage to England for the purpose of observing the progress there made in architecture and landscape gardening. Finding much in the public parks to enlist his sympathy and command attention, he was led by these experiences again, and more thoroughly, to advocate the idea he had already advanced, of a park for New York.

Accordingly, in 1851, Mr. A. C. Kingsland, then the mayor of the city, recommended to the common council that there should be prompt and efficient action taken upon the subject. This was the key-note from which the press and people took up the strain, and from that time it was a foregone conclusion that the people of New York must have a public park worthy the wants and fame of the metropolis.

After many vicissitudes of a legislative character, and much discussion as to the location, the legislature passed an act on the twenty-first of July 1853, authorizing the city to take possession of the ground now known as the Central Park.

The first commission for the Central Park, consisting of the mayor of the city and the street commissioner, was appointed May 19, 1856, and they, desiring advice and assistance in the discharge of their duties, invited a board of seven gentlemen, of which Washington Irving was President, to consult with them upon the measures to be taken whereby to effect the transformation of the land the city had acquired, for the purposes of the Park.

They proceeded to work upon a plan submitted by the engineer who made the original surveys; but it soon appearing that some change in the government of the work was essential to success, a new commission of eleven members was appointed, in April 1857, which board, by its successors, still controls the interests of the Park. The first act of the new commissioners was to advertise for new plans, and on the twenty-first of April, 1858, a selection was made from thirty-three plans submitted: the successful plan being the united work of Mr. Frederick Law Olmsted and Mr. Calvert Vaux. The wisdom of the commissioners is now apparent to all, in the successful fulfillment of the plan selected, which has been carried out in all its essential features, save at the upper end of the Park, where its extension from 106th to 110th streets rendered an entire modification necessary.

LOCATION AND AREA.

The Park occupies the paralellogram included within 59th Street on the south, 110th Street on the north, Fifth Avenue on the east, and Eighth Avenue on the west. The entire area is eight hundred and forty-three acres, of which one hundred and forty-one acres are occupied by the Croton Reservoirs, over forty-three acres by the waters of the Park, and of the remaining space one hundred and three acres are in drives, bridle-roads, and walks.

COST.

The original cost of the land   .   .   . $5,028,844
The total expenditure for construction from May
   1, 1857, to January 1, 1870 .   .   5,775,387

Total cost of the Park, January 1, 1870 $10,804,231

STATISTICS OF VISITORS.

The following record of attendance indicates the public appreciation of the Park: —

	Pedestrians.	Equestrians.	Vehicles.	Velocipedes.
1863,	1,469,335	90,724	922,450	
1864,	2,295,199	100,397	1,148,161	
1865,	3,219,056	98,360	1,425,241	
1866,	3,412,892	86,757	1,579,808	
1867,	2,998,770	84,994	1,381,697	
1868,	3,121,167	71,064	1,299,189	
1869,	3,265,541	54,611	1,340,697	8,714
1870,	3,494,877	75,511	1,616,935	234

The total number of persons that entered the Park during the year 1870, including drivers and occupants of carriages, was 8,421,427.

WHEN OPEN TO THE PUBLIC.

The Park is open daily to the public during the months of December, January, and February, from seven o'clock in the morning until eight o'clock in the evening; during the months of March, April, May, October, and November, from six o'clock in the morning until nine o'clock in the evening; and during the months of June, July, August, and September, from five o'clock in the morning until eleven o'clock in the evening.

CARRIAGE SERVICE.

Carriages, under the supervision of the commissioners, are run in the Park, whereby visitors may make a complete tour of the Park for twenty-five cents. Special information regarding them can always be had from the park-keepers in attendance at all hours. The usual point of starting is from the Merchant's Gate, Fifth Avenue and 59th Street. Time of the tour, one hour and a half.

GATEWAYS AND APPROACHES.

The greatest number of persons and carriages enter the Park by the Scholars' Gate, at the corner of Fifth Avenue and 59th Street — the natural entrance and exit of all arriving or departing by the Fifth Avenue. The improvements now in progress at this point, are rapidly making this gateway worthy of the noble avenue it adorns, and ere long it will be the most imposing of all the Park entrances; its surroundings include an open plaza on the opposite corner, which greatly heightens the effect by permitting a view of the Park for some distance down the avenue.

Next in importance, measured by the count of persons and vehicles entering it, is the Merchants' Gate at the corner of Eighth Avenue and 59th Street, the point where Broadway intersects the Eighth Avenue, and from which the grand boulevard departs in a northwesterly direction. To prevent the crowding and confusion that would naturally result from the concentration of so many leading thoroughfares at this locality, a grand circle has been laid out directly opposite the gateway, that contributes greatly to the general effect of this entrance to the Park.

After the gateways just described, the Farmers' and Warriors' gates on 110th Street, — the former at Sixth Avenue, and the latter at Seventh Avenue, — are of the greatest consequence. These two avenues are being converted into boulevards, which will be planted with double rows of trees, thus completing magnificent drives through Park and boulevard, from 59th Street to the Harlem River, thereby making these gates great means of ingress and egress for the pleasure-driving of the Park.

The improvements now being rapidly pushed forward on all the approaches to the Park, with that sleepless energy so indicative of the metropolitan spirit, are all arranged with special reference to its attractions, and will, ere long, form a fit setting for the city's gem.

The nomenclature of the gateways has been a subject of much interest; and the names selected happily illustrate the fact, that the Central Park is the people's pleasure-ground, common to all, regardless of rank or caste. There seems an especial fitness in the fact that in these titles, the young and old, art, literature, commerce, mechanics, and husbandry, all have a representation that will eventually find expression in the symbolic architecture of the completed gateways.

Herewith is a list of the names and locations of the several entrances : —

Fifth Avenue and 59th Street, The Scholars' Gate.
Sixth Avenue and 59th Street, The Artists' Gate.
Seventh Avenue and 59th Street, The Artizans' Gate.
Eighth Avenue and 59th Street, The Merchants' Gate.
Eighth Avenue and 72d Street, The Womens' Gate.
Eighth Avenue and 79th Street, The Hunters' Gate.

Eighth Avenue and 85th Street, The Mariners' Gate.
Eighth Avenue and 96th Street, The Gate of All-Saints.
Eighth Avenue and 100th Street, The Boys' Gate.
Fifth Avenue and 72d Street, The Childrens' Gate.
Fifth Avenue and 79th Street, The Miners' Gate.
Fifth Avenue and 90th Street, The Engineers' Gate.
Fifth Avenue and 96th Street, The Woodman's Gate.
Fifth Avenue and 102d Street, The Girls' Gate.
Fifth Avenue and 110th Street, The Pioneers' Gate.
Sixth Avenue and 110th Street, The Farmers' Gate.
Seventh Avenue and 110th Street, The Warriors' Gate.
Eighth Avenue and 110th Street, The Strangers' Gate.

THOROUGHFARES.

The regulations of the Park exclude all vehicles of a business nature from the pleasure drives; and to obviate the inconvenience incident to the interruption of travel across the city for so great a space, four transverse roads have been constructed for the accommodation of ordinary traffic, which are carried entirely across the Park by excavations below the level of the ground. So ingeniously have these road-ways been constructed that the visitor is scarcely aware of their existence, and, indeed, a remarkable aptness has been displayed in the arrangement of all the drives, bridle-paths, and walks, each being so independent of the other that the entire Park may be enjoyed either on foot, horseback, or in a carriage, without one class of visitors interfering with either of the others.

There are nine and one half miles of drives, varying in width from forty-five to sixty feet: there are five and one half miles of bridle paths of twenty-five feet width, and twenty-seven and one half miles of foot-walks, the latter following all the drives, but leading as well to many most beautiful spots, which are entirely lost to the visitor who only views the Park from a carriage.

THE CROTON RESERVOIRS.

These Reservoirs, so prominent in the scenery of the Park, and so important to the comfort and health of the city, were projected, and one of them completed, long before the occupation of the site for its present purposes. The Old or Lower Reservoir is a parallelogram in form, one thousand eight hundred and twenty-six feet long and eight hundred and thirty-five feet wide, covering an area of thirty-one acres, and capable of containing one hundred and fifty million gallons of water. It is divided into two sections, one with a depth of twenty, and the other of thirty feet. Its walls of solid masonry are twenty feet wide at the top, and gradually increase in thickness toward the base.

The Old Reservoir, being insufficient for the needs of the increasing population of the city, the New Reservoir was constructed simultaneously with the Park itself. It lies directly north of the other, and extends almost the entire width of the Park, having an irregular form, and an area of one hundred and six acres, with a maximum capacity of one thousand millions of gallons. The summits of the walls of both Reservoirs afford pleasant promenades and extensive views, while the skill of the architects and landscape gardeners has rendered the presence of that structure a source of satisfaction rather than of regret.

GENERAL FEATURES.

The Park is so naturally divided in two parts by the new or upper Reservoir, that by common consent the divisions are designated the Upper and Lower Park; which divisions we accept, and arrange the description accordingly.

It will only be our purpose to mention the several points of interest as they would be encountered in passing from the southern to the northern end of the Park, and not to follow any special route.

THE LOWER PARK.

This section of the Park is that lying below the new Reservoir, and is the portion upon which the larger amount of labor has been expended, in the adornment and improvement of the grounds. The leading features are the Mall, the Terrace, the Lake, and the Ramble; all of which, with the other leading points of interest, are noticed in the following pages.

THE HUMBOLDT MONUMENT.

The first object that attracts attention on entering the Park from Fifth Avenue and 59th Street, is the monument, surmounted by a life-size bust in bronze, of Alexander Von Humboldt, the work of Professor Blaiser, of Berlin, which was presented by the German citizens of New York. The unveiling of this monument on the fourteenth of September, 1869, the centennial anniversary of Von Humboldt's birth, was an occasion of great public interest.

THE STATUE OF COMMERCE.

Is placed near the Merchants' Gate, at the Eighth Avenue and 59th Street entrance. It was the gift of Mr. Stephen B.

Guion, a native of New York long resident in Liverpool, and is from the hand of Fosquet, a French artist of reputation and ability.

THE POND.

In the extreme southeastern angle of the Park, the Pond forms a pretty and leading feature in the scenery. It will be noticed on the left of the entrance by the Scholars' Gate. It has an extent of about five acres, and is largely artificial, being formed to a great degree by the natural drainage of the ground. In the winter season it is the resort of many skaters, its locality near the principal entrance making it more convenient of access than the larger Lake by the Terrace.

THE MUSEUM.

Another leading object that arrests attention in this portion of the Park is the old arsenal, a large and peculiar building near the Fifth Avenue boundary. It was formerly owned by the State, but was purchased by the city in 1856 for the sum of two hundred and seventy-five thousand dollars.

In and about this building, now more properly known as "The Museum," are kept the already large number of animals that form the nucleus of the collection for the Zoölogical Garden, now rapidly preparing in Manhattan Square, on Eighth Avenue, between 77th and 81st Streets, immediately opposite the western boundary of the Park; and which, when completed and stocked, will compare favorably with any similar institution in the world. The collection of animals is numerous, varied, and interesting, forming not the least of the many attractions of the Park.

In this building, also, is the beginning of the Museum of Natural History, which is destined to great prominence and usefulness. There are already many specimens of stuffed animals, and birds, and plans are being carried into practical realization, whereby, when proper accommodations have been provided at public expense, private liberality will supply specimens that will place this in the front rank of such collections.

Another feature of great importance within these walls, is the Meteorological Observatory, which finds accommodation in a large upper room, where a number of curious instruments record the doings of wind and weather. The ultimate intention is to add to this an Astronomical Observatory, when the necessary building shall have been provided.

It is also a part of the plans of the Commissioners to establish within the Park a permanent art gallery, but toward this end nothing has been done beyond the selection of a site for a building.

THE DAIRY.

Is a picturesque Gothic structure, situated directly north of the Pond and contiguous to the south transverse road, with which it is so connected that all supplies may be taken into it independently of the Park thoroughfares. Here pure milk, and similar refreshments more especially suited to the appetites of children, are supplied at a moderate cost.

A short distance from the Dairy, in an almost westerly direction, is

THE CHILDREN'S SUMMER-HOUSE,

Which opens upon a playground especially intended for the use of small children, where they may enjoy their little sports and neither interfere with, nor be molested by the rougher sports of

THE BOYS' PLAYGROUND,

Which is still further to the west, and occupies a large open space also south of transverse road No. 1. Here is a commodious house erected for the accommodation of the ball-players.

THE PALÆONTOLOGICAL MUSEUM.

The building for this purpose is now being erected near the Eighth Avenue, about midway between the Merchants' Gate and the first transverse road. The specimens for this department of natural history are being prepared by Professor B. Waterhouse Hawkins, and when the groups are completed will be extremely interesting, not only to scientists, but to ordinary visitors, as exhibiting the forms of extinct animal life in America.

THE MARBLE ARCH

Is located immediately west of the southern end of the Mall, and is one of the most elegant and costly structures within the Park, being the only one in which this material is exclusively used. Its purpose is to carry the carriage-drive over the foot-path, which enters it at one end on a level, while at the other a double stairway, leading to the right and left, leads up to the level of the Mall. On either side runs a marble bench that affords a welcome rest to the weary pedestrian on a hot summer day, and opposite the upper end of the arch, beyond the stairway, is a niche, around which, also, is a marble bench, and in its centre a drinking fountain.

THE GREEN.

Following the drive, that crosses the Marble Arch, as it leads to the west, and changes direction northward, a broad lawn of

2

fifteen acres, designated by name as the Green, is revealed.   In the proper season a large flock of South Down sheep, attended by a shepherd, find their pasture here, and supply a simple feature of rural life, at once beautiful and contrasting pleasantly with those other portions of the Park where art has done so much to beautify and please.

THE SPA

Is on the north side of the Green, and west of the Mall.   The building is highly decorated in arabesque.   Messrs. Schultz & Warker, the celebrated manufacturers of artificial mineral waters, are in charge, and supply the waters to visitors at five and ten cents per glass.

THE MALL.

The prominent feature of the Lower Park is the Mall; a straight walk which starts from a point just east of the Marble Arch and extends in a northerly direction for a distance of twelve hundred and twelve feet, nearly a quarter of a mile. The whole width is two hundred and eight feet; and throughout its entire length there is, on each side, a double row of American elms, separated by a promenade in the centre, of thirty-five feet in width.   Comfortable seats are distributed at convenient intervals, and drinking fountains at either end afford refreshment for the thirsty.   A statue of Shakespeare, the gift of a number of citizens of New York through the Shakespeare Dramatic Association, is to be placed at the southeast corner of the walk. The Mall terminates at the northern end in a spacious square or plaza, which is ornamented with two very pretty fountains, and gilded bird-cages mounted on pedestals.   On music days, when the sun is oppressive, this space is covered with an awning and provided with seats where visitors may rest, enjoy the music, and indulge in the luxury of creams and ices from the adjacent Casino.   In close proximity to this plaza, and east of the north end of the Mall, is

THE MUSIC STAND,

An elaborate structure, decorated with gilding and bright colors, from which, on Saturday afternoons in the summer and autumn, .an excellent band discourses beautiful music.   Our illustration gives the grouping of the scene at this point, including the north end of the Mall and the Music Stand.

THE TREES PLANTED BY THE PRINCE OF WALES

During his visit to this country in the autumn of 1860, — an English oak and an American elm, — are thriving finely.   They may be found west of the centre of the Mall, between the foot-path and drive.

THE VINERY

Is a delightful bower of rustic work over which are trained wisterias, honeysuckle, and rose vines. It is situated just east of the upper end of the Mall, convenient to the Music Pavilion and the Casino, at a point commanding an excellent view of the Terrace, Lake, and Ramble.

THE MALL FROM TERRACE.

THE CARRIAGE CONCOURSE

Is an open square adjoining the Vinery, affording visitors in carriages access to the Casino, and is a convenient place to pause on music days and enjoy the band without alighting.

THE CASINO

Is a neat and tasteful cottage structure designed for a ladies' refreshment house, where a well ordered restaurant is maintained, and although a private business, like the Refectory at Mount St. Vincent, is still under the supervision and control of the Park Commissioners. The Casino is pleasantly located just at the edge of the Carriage Concourse, and overlooking all the attractions of the Terrace and vicinity.

THE BRONZE STATUE OF THE TIGRESS

May be found a short distance west of the Terrace, to the right of the drive. It represents a tigress in the act of bringing food to her cubs, and was presented to the Park by twelve gentlemen, residents of New York. It is six feet high, seven and a half feet long, and is the production of the celebrated Auguste Caine.

THE TERRACE.

Dividing the plaza that terminates the Mall from the carriage drive that intervenes between it and the Terrace, is a magnificent screen work of Albert freestone, in which are two openings whereby persons can leave their carriages and enter the Mall, or from it can cross the drive to the stairways that lead to the Terrace below. These stairs, which are displayed in the frontispiece, are worthy of the closest examination, for it will be seen that no two of the many panels that surround the well of the staircase are alike, and it is their beauty and ingenuity rather than mere variety that make them objects of admiration. The decoration is all based upon forms of vegetation symbolic of the four seasons, and surpasses the decorative sculpture on any public building in America.

Pursuant to the theory that every visitor, whether walking, riding, or driving, may visit the entire Park in his own way without interference, another means of access from the Mall to the Terrace has been provided, so that drivers may not be embarrassed by pedestrians crossing the roadway at this much thronged point, and they, in turn, may not be exposed to the risks thereby incurred. To meet this end, a stairway has been constructed from the plaza at the end of the Mall to the level of the Terrace below, terminating in an arcade that passes under the drive. The floor and ceiling are finished in elaborate patterns of encaustic tiles, and the stone work is everywhere beautifully carved. The plan for the hall or arcade, for the stairways leading to it, as well as for the stairway from the drive to the Terrace, embraces many artistic embellishments that cannot be carried into effect for some years to come.

Having passed over one or the other of the stairways leading from the upper level the visitor reaches the Terrace, a broad esplanade which stretches north to the margin of the Lake. It is inclosed with a low wall of carved stone which is pierced with three openings, one on either side, from which foot-paths lead northward, and one on the water front whence visitors may take the boats for a row on the Lake.

In the centre is a fountain — a picture of which is here presented — with a spacious basin, still incomplete (there being certain bronze castings for its ornamentation to arrive from Munich), yet beautiful and very attractive. At either corner on the water front is a tall mast, from one of which floats a standard with the arms of the State, while the other bears a similar emblem with the arms of the city.

THE LAKE.

From the Terrace the attention is turned naturally toward the Lake, frequently mentioned as the Central Lake. This sheet of water stretches away from the front of the Terrace to the west and north, in an eccentric outline of bays and headlands, which, with the little. islands that dot the surface, the dense woods of

FOUNTAIN ON LOWER TERRACE.

the eastern and northern shore, the elaborate Terrace on the southern side, the boats, swans, and ducks floating upon the surface, combine to produce a most picturesque effect. The Lake is divided into two unequal parts by the Bow Bridge, an iron structure so called from its form, which connects the foot-path on the southerly side with the Ramble on the opposite shore. West from this bridge is the larger portion of the Lake, and farther away to the west the Balcony Bridge, illustrated by the cut upon the next page, crosses a small arm of the Lake at a point near Eighth Avenue and 77th Street. The swans are not the least interesting feature of the Lake. Twelve of them were originally the gift of the city of Hamburg. Nine of these dying, twelve more were presented from the same source, to which were added fifty from some gentlemen in London. Of the original seventy-two twenty-eight died, and the remainder with their progeny remain to do the elegant upon the Lake. The swans, and also the white ducks that bear them company, are very tame, and come readily at a call. The popularity of the boats upon the Lake is evident from the fact that, during the year 1869, no less than one hundred and twenty-six thousand persons availed themselves of the opportunity for this amusement. There are two classes of boats, the omnibus, which sail at fixed rates of fare for the

BALCONY BRIDGE.

round trip, and the call boats that go at the pleasure of the passengers. The charges are moderate, and the remuneration to the lessee quite small for so extensive a business. The boats may be taken from the Terrace, and may be left at any one of the six pretty boat-houses that adorn the shore of the Lake. These are exceedingly tasteful structures, as will appear from the illustration given upon the next page.

It is, however, in the winter season that the Lake, and other waters of the Park furnish attraction to the greatest numbers. The care exercised that the ice may be properly kept in order for skating purposes, is fully appreciated by the many thousands that throng to the Park when "the ball" is up, and where under a few simple and reasonable restrictions any one may come and enjoy this exhilarating winter sport. The northern end of the western portion of the Lake is reserved exclusively for ladies.

BOAT-HOUSE ON LAKE.

The Scotch citizens of New York here find opportunity to enjoy their national game of curling. This game is growing greatly in popularity under the encouragement and approval of the Park Commissioners. Commodious houses are erected in the winter season on the margin of the Lake for the accommodation and refreshment of spectators, skaters, and curlers. They are so constructed as to be readily removed at the close of the season.

THE RAMBLE.

, After the Lake, the Ramble is the natural attraction. It cov-
ers a piece of ground of about thirty-six acres sloping upward
from the northern shore of the lake to the old Croton Reservoir,
and is bounded on either side by the great drive, from which
access may be gained by foot-paths that leave the drive at the
northwest and northeast corners of the Ramble, although the
principal avenue of approach is by the Bow Bridge across
the narrow part of the Lake. The Ramble is a labyrinth of
wooded walks abounding in sequestered nooks, rustic bridges
over little brooks, wild vines and flowers, summer-houses and
seats of rustic make, occasional little patches of lawn, all cluster-
ing so naturally that the agency of art in the grouping scarce
seems apparent. It is not surprising that the Ramble has more
loving friends than any other portion of the Park, when it is con-
sidered how many are the attractions it offers. The Lake shore
is beautiful at every point; fine views everywhere reveal themselves; foreign birds, as pelicans, storks, cranes, and herons, have
here their home; and for the pleasant chat of friends, the quiet
enjoyment of a book, or simple rest from toil, the Ramble has
abundant accommodation. More pretentious descriptions than
this utterly fail of justice to its beauties. To be enjoyed it
must be visited; to be appreciated it must be made one's own
familiar friend.

THE MONUMENT TO SCHILLER,

The German poet, is placed in the western part of the Ramble,
near the shore of the northern arm of the Lake.

THE CAVE.

At the base of the extreme western slope of the Ramble is the
Cave, an interesting spot, partly natural and partly artificial. A
steep path leads to the foot of a large rock, turning which sharp
to the left the cave is entered at a level; the entrance is dark,
but a few steps reveal the light, and afford an outlook upon the
Lake. From the other side a series of rocky steps lead to the
top of the rock over the Cave.

THE BELVEDERE

Is an irregular Gothic structure situated on a large rock that
pierces the wall of the old Reservoir at its southwestern angle.
This rock was long an eye-sore in this portion of the Park, but
has now been put to the excellent purpose of sustaining an ad-

ditional and attractive feature of the landscape, which not only provides a pleasant place of rest and shelter, but is an excellent post of observation, the rock itself being the highest point in the Park.

THE TUNNEL

Has been excavated through the rock just south of the Belvedere and north of the Ramble, for the accommodation of the traffic road that crosses the Park at 79th Street. It is one hundred and forty-six feet long, and seventeen feet ten inches high. It is chiefly interesting as illustrating the great expenditure of time, labor, and money necessary to perfect the attractions of the Park.

CONSERVATORY LAKE.

Conservatory Lake is an ornamental piece of water, of two acres in extent, lying contiguous to the Fifth Avenue, directly east of the Lake, and is a feature of a charming plan, embracing both conservatory and flower-garden, now rapidly approaching completion.

THE DOVE COTES

Are directly north of Conservatory Lake, by the foot-path that runs nearest to the Fifth Avenue. They are a very pretty conceit, and add much to the beauty of the Park in this vicinity. The bird houses are elevated upon tall posts, and the whole inclosed in an immense wire cage or screen work.

THE EVERGREEN WALK,

Near the Fifth Avenue, and south of the entrance by the Miners' Gate at 79th Street, a pretty piece of landscape gardening, was first laid out in 1862. It increases in interest and importance with the growth of the trees, and includes circles within circles of walks, inclosed by neatly trimmed hedges, the whole encircled by a thicket of shrubbery and trees that serves to conceal the plan of the walks within.

THE SITE FOR THE ART MUSEUM

The proposed Art Museum is to be located north of the transverse road at 79th Street, and near the Fifth Avenue. The plan contemplates an extensive and elegant structure.

THE CEDARS,

At the intersection of the drive and transverse road, near the southeast corner of the old Reservoir, is a point of interest worthy of observation.

THE MAZE

Is a recently completed feature of the Park, and is located near the southeastern corner of the old Reservoir. Included within the inclosure are thirty-seven hundred feet of gravel walk, and twenty-two hundred and fifty trees, as borders or screens, the object of which is to render an attempt to reach its central point, or to find a place of exit somewhat amusing and difficult. When the trees are sufficiently grown to conceal the paths, the Maze will be a source of much amusement.

MANHATTAN SQUARE,

Now being prepared for the Zoölogical Gardens, is west of the Park, on the 8th Avenue, between 77th and 81st streets.

THE KNOLL,

Or, as sometimes called, Summit Rock, is in the extreme western portion of the Park, opposite the upper section of the old Reservoir. Being of easy ascent, its height is quite deceptive; but it well repays the trouble of a visit, as it commands one of the most extensive views to be had in the Park.

THE UPPER PARK

All of that portion of the Park lying north of the New Reservoir is usually known as the Upper Park, but is connected with the Lower Park by the drive, bridle-road, and foot-path. This section has not received the amount of elaboration that has been bestowed upon the Lower Park, but should not on that account be neglected by the visitor. The special objects of interest are not numerous; but the landscape has a bold, free character, the drives have longer sweeps and stretches, the elevations and depressions are more marked, and the views from the higher points abundantly reward the time, trouble, and strength consumed in seeking them. The most prominent features will be found noted in detail in the following pages.

MOUNT ST. VINCENT.

The thoroughfares that lead from the Lower Park pass entirely around a large, open space, north of the New Reservoir, denominated the East and West Meadows, the roadway on the east side leading beyond to Mount St. Vincent. The building here located was formerly used for the Roman Catholic Academy, now on the Hudson near Yonkers. It is used principally for a restaurant, where may be found at all times comfortable rest and refreshment. The remainder of the building is occupied by offices of the Park, and a Museum in which are deposited the casts of the late Mr. Crawford's sculptures, eighty-seven in all, which were presented to the Park, by his widow, in 1860.

OLD FORTIFICATIONS.

Well to the northeast corner of the Park, and forming a pretty point from which to overlook the Harlem Meer, are the remains of earthworks erected during the war of 1812. They have been neatly turfed over, but preserved as nearly as possible in their original form.

THE BLOCK-HOUSE.

Considerably to the west of the earthworks, beyond the Lake and near the Warrior's Gate, which opens upon Seventh Avenue, is a small block-house, a relic of 1812, and which was used either as a magazine or fortification. This and the earthworks were links in the chain of fortifications that extended across the north end of the island, of which abundant evidences exist further to the west.

THE POOL, LOCH, AND HARLEM MEER.

The three bodies of water bearing the above names, are essentially one, being connected and flowing into each other. Like the other waters of the Park, they are mainly artificial, formed to a great extent by collecting the drainage of the valley that here traverses the entire Park diagonally. The waters flow from the Pool, that begins within a few feet of the wall on the west at 101st Street, to the Harlem Meer, that reaches within a few feet of the eastern boundary from 107th to 110th Streets, and follows the northern line from the corner to a point midway between the Sixth and Seventh avenues. A small streamlet connects the Pool on the west with the Loch in the centre, and another little run connects the Loch with the Meer on the east. A foot-path runs around the entire water, winding over romantic bridges by foaming little cascades and quiet pools. We can only hint at these points and leave the seeker for the beauties of the Park to find and enjoy them for himself.

THE NURSERY.

The Nursery lies near the Fifth Avenue boundary, south of the Harlem Meer, and east of Mount St. Vincent.

It is expected eventually to extend this arboretum, so that it may include specimens of all American trees that flourish north of the Carolinas, grown singly and in groups. At present, however, the space occupied is simply used as a nursery.

THE GREAT HILL.

This elevation, about midway between the Pool and the northern boundary, is a central feature in the northwestern portion of the Park. Its altitude is not quite so great as the Knoll, but from the greater depressions about it appears much higher. There is a carriage concourse at the top, whence there is a commanding view, extending from the Hudson to the East River and the Sound, including within its scope a remarkable variety of feature and interesting incident.

THE HIGH BRIDGE.

This is the most important structure connected with the Croton Aqueduct, the great canal that conducts the water supply of New York City, from the Croton River, a distance of over forty miles, to the great receiving Reservoir. The High Bridge crosses the Harlem River and Valley, a distance of fourteen hundred and fifty feet. It has eight arches of eighty feet span, and one hundred feet in height, from the river to the lower side. It may be crossed by a foot-path, and is a point of interest not to be omitted by the tourist. It can be reached by the Harlem Railroad, or in summer by the Third Avenue Railroad to Harlem, and thence by steamboat.

PUBLIC SQUARES AND PARKS.

THE various Public Parks of the city, the names and location of which are noted below, are, under the judicious management of the Park Commissioners, becoming constantly more beautiful and interesting. In addition to the improved appearance of these squares, the Commissioners have introduced music in the various parks at stated intervals during the summer season. The times and places of these performances are announced in the daily press, as they occur.

THE BATTERY.

On the southwestern water front of the city, the Battery has an area of about twelve acres and a fine growth of trees. On the grounds is an old fortification, known as Castle Garden, which for a long while served as a place of amusement, but is now a landing-place for emigrants; an unsightly building, only to be tolerated for the useful purpose it serves.

THE BOWLING GREEN.

A small inclosure at the foot of Broadway, is of no special interest beyond the historic fact that it formerly contained a leaden statue of George III., which the patriotic citizens destroyed and converted into musket balls, during the Revolutionary War.

THE CITY HALL PARK

Is triangular in form, facing Broadway between Ann and Chambers streets. Its original area was eleven acres, of which a portion has been cut off for the new Post Office. It contains the City Hall, the new Court House and other smaller public buildings.

WASHINGTON SQUARE,

Formerly the Potter's Field, containing nine acres, lies between Waverly Place on the north and Fourth Street on the south. It is bisected by the extension of Fifth Avenue, the passage of which through the square has been ornamented by a handsome fountain.

UNION SQUARE

Extends across the head of Broadway, between 14th and 17th streets. On the south of this square, on the eastern side, is the bronze equestrian statue of Washington, and on the western side the bronze statue of Lincoln.

GRAMERCY PARK

Is a private property, lying between 20th and 21st streets and the Third and Fourth avenues.

STUYVESANT PARK

Lies on either side of Second Avenue between 15th and 17th streets. St. George's Episcopal Church is on the west side of the park.

TOMPKINS SQUARE

Is between Avenues A and B, and 7th and 8th streets. It is one of the largest parks in the city, and is much used for military purposes.

MADISON SQUARE

Is at the junction of Fifth Avenue and Broadway, and has an area of ten acres. On the west side stands the monument to General Worth.

RESERVOIR SQUARE

Is between Fifth and Sixth avenues, and 40th and 42d streets. The distributing reservoir occupies one half its area, and the remainder, formerly the site of the Crystal Palace, is now kept as an open park.

MOUNT MORRIS SQUARE

Is at Fifth Avenue and 120th Street. Its area is nearly twenty acres, and is quite a resort for the citizens of Harlem.

MANHATTAN SQUARE,

On 8th Avenue, between 77th and 81st streets, is now being arranged for zoölogical grounds of the Central Park.

HAMILTON SQUARE

Extends from the Third to the Fifth Avenue, between 66th and 68th streets, opposite the eastern boundary of the Central Park.

PUBLIC BUILDINGS.

THE CITY HALL

Is situated in the park that bears its name, and was erected during the years 1803-10. The cupola was destroyed by fire in 1859, on the occasion of the Atlantic Cable celebration. It was, however, immediately rebuilt, and the former clock replaced by one of superior construction, the time of which is so accurate that it is accepted as standard by the business community of the city. The Mayor, Common Council, Aldermen, and other public officials have offices in the building, which also contains the Governor's room and the City Library.

THE NEW COURT HOUSE

This extensive building — still unfinished, but sufficiently complete to admit of its occupancy — is located in the City Hall Park, at the rear of the City Hall and fronting on Chambers street. Its dimensions are two hundred and fifty feet in length by one hundred and fifty in breadth, and the total height, when completed, will be two hundred and twenty-five feet. The building is entirely fire-proof, and within its walls are accommodations for the County Clerk, Register, Surrogate, Sheriff, Comptroller, and City Chamberlain. The work was commenced in 1861, and has already cost nearly $5,000,000. Its architectural beauties will surpass any other structure in the city, and it will well repay a visit.

THE POST OFFICE

In Nassau Street, between Cedar and Liberty streets, was formerly the Middle Dutch Church. It is a very old building, and suffered much injury at the hands of the British during the Revolutionary War. It was subsequently repaired, and for a time devoted to religious uses, but was afterwards purchased by the Government for its present purpose.

POST OFFICE REGULATIONS.

Cedar, corner Nassau.

Office Hours. — This office is open continuously, except Sundays. Sundays, from 9 to 10 A. M., and from 12.30 to 1.30 P. M.

There are eight deliveries each day by carriers.

Collections are made from each and every lamp-post box (five hundred and eighty-five in number) nine times a day.

On Sundays but one collection will be made, at 3 15 P. M.

U. S. MAIL STATIONS.

Open from 6.30 A. M. to 9.30 P. M.

A, 100 Spring St.   H, Third Av. near E. 58th St.
B, 382 Grand St.   J, Harsenville.
C, 627 Hudson St.   K, E. 86th, near Third Av.
D, Bible House.   L, 2277 Third Av.
E, 304 Eighth Av.   M, Carmansville.
F, 342 Third Av.   N, Tubby Hook.
G, 735 Seventh Av.

MONEY ORDER DEPARTMENT.
Entrance on Cedar Street.

Office hours from 10 A. M. to 3 P. M.

THE NEW POST OFFICE

Is now in course of construction on the triangular piece of ground formed by the running of a new street across the lower portion of the City Hall Park. Some time must elapse before the building will be in a sufficient state of forwardness to be an object of especial interest to the stranger visiting New York.

THE TOMBS,

Or more properly The Halls of Justice, occupy the block bounded by Centre, Elm, Franklin, and Leonard streets, fronting on the first named. It is a massive structure in the Egyptian style, completed in 1838, and accommodates the Police Court, Court of Sessions, and the City Prison. Visitors are admitted on application to the keeper.

THE CUSTOM HOUSE

Was originally constructed for the Merchants' Exchange. It is located in Wall Street, and fills the block between William and Hanover streets. Its dimensions are two hundred feet in length, and from one hundred and forty-four to one hundred and seventy-one feet in breadth, with an elevation of one hundred and twenty-four feet to the top of the dome. It is entirely devoted to the business pertaining to the custom service.

THE UNITED STATES SUB-TREASURY AND ASSAY OFFICE

Is on Wall Street, at the corner of Nassau, extending through the block with a front on Pine Street. It is a spacious, substantial, and beautiful building, of white marble, after the model of the

3

Parthenon at Athens. This building was formerly the Custom House, but was devoted to its present use upon the removal of the latter to the Merchants' Exchange. Visitors are admitted to witness the operations of the Assay Office on Wednesdays between the hours of ten and twelve A. M.

THE COOPER UNION

Is a spacious and elegant building occupying the entire block between Third and Fourth avenues and Seventh and Eighth streets. It was erected by Mr. Peter Cooper for the " moral, intellectual, and physical improvement of his countrymen; " and presented by him to a board of directors to manage and control for the benefit of the public. The cost of the building was about $300,000, and the income from the rented portion is from $25,000 to $30,000 per annum. In the basement is a large hall or lecture-room; on the first and second floors are stores and offices. The remainder of the building is devoted to the purposes of the Institute, which embrace instruction in various branches, — a library, reading-room, and course of lectures — all free.

THE NATIONAL ACADEMY OF DESIGN

Has a new building at the northwest corner of the Fourth Avenue and 23d Street. This building is a peculiar structure, embodying many points of interest that reward careful study and examination. The annual exhibitions of the Academy are held during the months of April, May, June, and July; and include only the works of living artists, and such pictures as have not previously been exhibited in New York. The annual exhibition of the Artists' Fund Society is usually held in this building during the months of November and December.

THE YOUNG MENS' CHRISTIAN ASSOCIATION BUILDING.

This edifice is at the southwest corner of Fourth Avenue and 23d Street. It is spacious, complete, elegant, and admirably adapted to its purpose.

EQUITABLE LIFE INSURANCE BUILDING.
Broadway, corner of Liberty Street.

NEW YORK LIFE INSURANCE BUILDING.
Broadway, corner of Leonard Street.

PARK BANK BUILDING.
Broadway, between Fulton and Ann Streets.

No visitor to New York desiring to see the objects of interest in the city should regard a visit complete without seeing the above named buildings, and the elegant business offices of the several companies owning them.

———◇———

CHURCHES.

BAPTIST.

Abyssinian (colored), 166 Waverly Place. Rev. W. Spelman, Minister.

Amity St., West 54th St. near 8th Avenue.

Antioch, 278 Bleecker St.

Berean, 35 Downing St. Rev. P. L. Davis, Minister.

Bloomingdale, 220 West 42d St.

Calvary, 50 West 23d St. Rev. R. J. McArthur, Minister.

Central Park, East 83d St. near Second Avenue. Rev. C. C. Norton, Minister.

East Madison, cor. Gouverneur St. Rev. John Quincy Adams, Minister.

Ebenezer, 154 West 36th St. Rev. William Thorp, Minister.

Fifth Avenue, 6 West 46th St. Rev. Thomas Armitage, Minister.

Fifth Avenue, near West 126th St. Rev. Elijah Lucas, Minister.

First, Park Avenue cor. East 39th St. Rev. Thomas D. Anderson, Minister.

First German, East 14th St. near First Avenue. Rev. H. M. Schaffer, Minister.

First Mariner's, Oliver cor. Henry St. Rev. J. L. Hodge, Minister.

Freewill Baptist, 104 West 17th St. Rev. C. E. Blake, Minister.

Hope Chapel, East 111th St. near Third Avenue.

Laight Street, cor. Varick St. Rev. Frederick E. Evans, Minister.

McDougal Street, 22 McDougal St. Rev. William Reed, Minister.

Madison Avenue, cor. East 31st St. Rev. —— Elder, Minister.

Murray Hill, Lexington Avenue, cor. East 37th St. Rev. Sidney A. Corey, Minister.

North, 126 Christopher St.

Pilgrim, West 33d St. near 8th Avenue. Rev. W. H. Felix, Minister.

Plymouth, West 51st St. near Ninth Avenue. Rev. Isaac Wescott, Minister.

Second German, 451 West 45th St. Rev. Henry Schneider, Minister.

Sixth Street, 644 Sixth St. Rev. Henry Angell, Minister.
Sixteenth Street, 257 West 16th St. Rev. W. S. Mikels, Minister.
South, 235 West 25th St. Rev. —— Stevens, Minister.
Stanton Street, 36 Stanton St. Rev. C. Rhodes, Minister.
Tabernacle, 166 Second Avenue. Rev. J. R. Kendrick, Minister.
Welsh, 141 Chrystie St.
West 53d St., near Seventh Avenue. Rev. W. H. Pendleton, Minister.

CONGREGATIONAL.

Church of the Pilgrims, 365 West 48th St.
East 125th St., near Second Avenue. Rev. S. Bourne, Minister.
New England, 489 Fifth Avenue. Rev. J. M. Sturtevant, Minister.
Tabernacle, Sixth Avenue cor. West 34th St. Rev. J. P. Thompson, Minister.
Welsh, 206 East 11th St.
West 50th St., near Eighth Avenue.

FRIENDS.

East 15th St., cor. Rutherford Place.
Twentieth Street, East 20th St. near Third Avenue.
Twenty-Seventh Street, 43 West 27th St.

JEWISH SYNAGOGUES.

Adas Jeshurun, West 39th Street, near Seventh Avenue. D. Einhorn, Rabbi.
Adereth El, 135 East 20th St. Morris Leon, President.
Ahavath Chesed, Avenue C, cor. East 4th St. Ignatz Stein, President.
Anshi Chesed, 146 Norfolk St. S. Schuster, President; M. Mielziner, Rabbi.
Beth Cholim, 232 West 28th St.
Beth El, 248 West 33d St. L. Borchard, President.
Beth Hamedrash, 78 Allen St.
Beth Hamedrash 2d, 153 Chatham St.
Beth Israel Bikur Cholim, 56 Chrystie St. N. Cowen, President.
Bikur Cholim, U. Kadisha, 63 Chrystie St.
Bnai Israel, 41 Stanton St. S. L. Garritts, President.
Bnai Jeshurun, 145 West 34th St. H. Davidson, President; H Vidaver, Rabbi Preacher.
Bnai Sholom, Third St. cor. Avenue C. C. M. Gerber, President.
Chisuk Amuno, East 54th St. near Third Avenue.
Dareeh Amuno, 164 Greene St. A. Oettinger, President.
Mischkan Israel, 112 East 12th St.

Poel Zedeck, West 29th St. cor. Eighth Avenue.
Rodeph Schoelm, 8 Clinton St. R. Goldschmidt, President.
Shaarai Berocho, 306 Sixth St. A. Menzel, President.
Shaarai Rach Mim, 156 Attorney St. M. Fleishauer, President.
Shaarai Tephila, West 44th St. near Broadway. B. L. Solomon,
President; S. M. Isaacs, Minister.
Shaarai Zedeck, 38 Henry St. E. Japha, President.
Shaaer Hashamoin, 91 Rivington St. L. Samuels, President.
Shagnarai Tikva, East 87th St. near Third Avenue.
Shearith Israel, 114 Columbia St. M. Westheimer, President.
Shearith Israel, West 19th St. near Fifth Avenue. A. R. B.
Moses. President; J. J. Lyons, Minister.
Temple, Fifth Avenue, cor. East 43d St. L. May, President;
Samuel Adler, Rabbi; A. Rubin, Reader.

LUTHERAN.

Gustavus Adolphus, 151 East 22d St.
Holy Trinity, 47 West 21st St. Rev. G. F. Krotel, Minister.
Immanuel, East 83d St. near Third Avenue.
Immanuel, East 87th St. near Third Avenue. Rev. L. Haffman,
Minister.
Lutheran, Avenue B, cor. East 9th St. Rev. F. W. Foehlinger,
Minister.
St. James', 216 East 15th St. Rev. A. C. Wedekind, Minister.
St. John's, East 127th St. near Fourth Avenue.
St. John's, 81 Christopher St. Rev. A. H. M. Held, Minister.
St. Luke's, 318 West 43d St. Rev. G. W. Drees, Minister.
St. Marcus', 323 Sixth Street. Rev. H. Ragener, Minister.
St. Matthew's, 354 Broome St. Rev. G. Norberg, Minister.
St. Paul's, 226 Sixth Avenue. Rev. F. W. Geisenhainer, Min-
ister.
St. Paul's, West 123d St. near Seventh Avenue. Rev. J. Ehr-
hart, Minister.
St. Peter's, 145 East 50th St. C. Hennicke, Minister.

METHODIST EPISCOPAL

Presiding Elders. — New York District, W. H. Ferris; New
York East District, H. F. Pease.

Alanson, 52 Norfolk St.
Allen Street, 126 Allen St.
Bedford Street, 28 Morton St.
Beekman Hill, 321 East 50th St.
Bethel Ship, foot of Carlisle St.
Central, 58 Seventh Avenue.
Chapel, Broadway corner of West 68th St.
Duane Street, 294 Hudson St.

Eighteenth Street, 307 West 18th St.
Eleventh Street Chapel, 545 East 11th St.
Fifty-Third Street, 231 West 53d St.
Forsyth Street, 10 Forsyth St.
Forty-Fourth Street, 461 West 44th St.
Forty-Third Street, 253 West 43d St.
German, 252 Second St.
German, 346 West 40th St.
Greene Street, 59 Greene St.
Harlem, East 125th St. near Third Avenue.
Hedding, 337 East 17th St.
Jane Street, 13 Jane St.
John Street, 44 John St.
Ladies' Five Points Home Mission, 71 Park St.
Lexington Avenue. cor. East 52d St.
Perry Street, 122 Perry St.
Rose Hill, 221 East 27th St.
St. Paul's, Fourth Avenue cor. East 22d St.
Second Avenue, cor. East 119th St.
Second Street, 276 Second St.
Seventh Street, 24 Seventh St.
Sixty-First Street Chapel, East 61st St. near Third Avenue.
Thirtieth Street, 331 West 30th St.
Thirty-Fifth Street, West 35th St, near 10th Avenue.
Thirty-Seventh Street, 223 East 37th St.
Trinity, 248 West 34th St.
Twenty-Fourth Street, 359 West 24th St.
Washington Square, 137 West 4th St.
West Harlem, West 125th St. near 6th Avenue.
Willett Street, 7 Willett St.
Yorkville, 115 East 86th St.

AFRICAN METHODIST EPISCOPAL.

African Union, 161 West 15th St.
Bethel, 214 Sullivan St.
Little Zion, East 117th St. near Second Avenue.
Zion, 351 Bleecker St.

PRESBYTERIAN.

Alexander, 127 Seventh Avenue.
Allen Street, 61 Allen St. Rev. W. W. Newell, Minister.
Brick, Fifth Avenue cor. West 37th St. Rev. Gardner Spring, Minister: Rev. J. O. Murray, colleague.
Central, West 56th St. near Broadway. Rev. J. D. Wilson, Minister.
Chelsea, 353 West 22d St. Rev. Morse Rowell, Minister.

Church of the Covenant. Fourth Avenue cor. East 35th St. Rev. George L. Prentiss, Minister.

Church of the Covenant (colored), 138 Laurens St. Rev. Thomas C. Oliver, Minister.

Church of the Sea and Land, Market St. cor. Henry St. Rev. E. Hopper, Minister.

Eighty-Fourth Street, near Bloomingdale Road.

Eleventh, East 55th St. near Lexington Avenue. Rev. C. S. Robinson, Minister.

Fifth Avenue, cor. East 19th St. Rev. John Hall, Minister.

First, Fifth Avenue cor. West 11th St. Rev. W. M. Paxton, Minister.

First Union, 145 East 83th St.

Fortieth Street, East 40th St. near Lexington Avenue. Rev. John E. Annan, Minister.

Forty-Second Street, 233 West 42d St.

Fourth Avenue, 288 Fourth Avenue. Rev. Howard Crosby, Minister.

Fourteenth Street, cor. Second Avenue. Rev. E. W. Hitchcock, Minister.

Fourth, 124 West 34th St. Rev. John Thompson, Minister.

French Evangelical, 9 University Place.

German, 290 Madison St. Rev. B. Krusi, Minister.

German Evangelical.

Harlem, East 127th St. near Third Avenue.

Irish, 17 Greene St. Rev. David Mitchell, Minister.

Lexington Avenue, cor. East 46th St. Rev. J. Sanderson, Minister.

Madison Square, Madison Avenue cor. East 24th St. Rev. William Adams, Minister.

Manhattanville, West 126th St. cor. Ninth Avenue.

Mount Washington, near King's Bridge. Rev. R. W. Dickinson, Minister.

North, Ninth Avenue cor. West 31st St. Rev. Thomas Street, Minister.

Phillips, Madison Avenue cor. East 73d St. Rev. S. D. Alexander, Minister.

Rutgers, Madison Avenue cor. East 29th St. Rev. N. W. Conkling, Minister.

Scotch, 53 West 14th St. Rev. Joseph McElroy, Minister; Rev. M. C. Sutphen, colleague.

Seventh, Broome St. cor. Ridge St. Rev. T. M. Dawson, Minister.

Shiloh (colored), 61 Prince St.

Spring Street, 246 Spring St. Rev. Wm. Aikman, Minister.

Thirteenth Street, 145 West 13th St. Rev. S. D. Burchard, Minister.

Twenty-Third Street, 210 West 23d St. Rev. H. D. Northrup, Minister.

University Place, cor. East 10th St. Rev. A. H. Kellogg, Minister.

Washington Heights. Rev. Charles A. Stoddard, Minister.

West Houston. cor. Thompson St. Rev. W. W. Page, Minister.

West, 31 West 42d St. Rev. Thomas S. Hastings, Minister.

Westminster, 151 West 22d St. Rev. G. M. McEckron, Minister.

UNITED PRESBYTERIAN.

Eleventh Street, 206 East 11th St.

First, East 116th St. near Second Avenue.

Jane Street, 41 Jane St. Rev. Geo. D. Mathews' Minister.

Seventh Avenue, 29 Seventh Avenue.

Third, 41 Charles St. Rev. Hugh H. Blair, Minister.

West Forty-Fourth Street, 434 West 44th St. Rev. G. Campbell, Minister.

West Twenty Fifth Street, 161 West 25th St. Rev. Jas. Thompson, Minister.

REFORMED PRESBYTERIAN.

First, 123 West 12th St. Rev. J. N. McLeod, Minister.

First, 426 West 28th St. Rev. J. C. K. Milligan, Minister.

Second, Second Avenue cor. East 11th St. Rev. Geo. S. Chambers, Minister

Second, 167 West 11th St.

Third, 238 West 23d St.

PROTESTANT EPISCOPAL.

Right Rev. Horatio Potter, Bishop.

Advent, 55 West 46th St. Rev. A. B. Hart, Rector.

All Angels, 81st St. cor. Eleventh Avenue. Rev. J. M. Heffernan, Rector.

All Saints, 286 Henry St. Rev. S. J. Corneille. Rector.

Annunciation, 142 West 14th St. Rev. W. J. Seabury. Rector.

Ascension, Fifth Avenue cor. West 10th St. Rev. John Cotton Smith, Rector.

Atonement, Madison Avenue cor. East 28th St. Rev. W. T. Sabine, Rector.

Calvary, Fourth Avenue cor. East 21st St. Rev. E. A. Washburn, Rector.

Chapel of Saint Chrysostom, Seventh Avenue cor. West 39th St. Rev. Thos. H. Sill. Rector.

Chapel of the Comforter, East 44th St. cor. Third Avenue.

Chapel of the Holy Comforter, 75 Beach St.

Chapel of the Holy Saviour, East 25th St. near Madison Avenue. Rev. A. B. Carter, Rector.

Church of the Holy Light, 437 Seventh Avenue. Rev. E. Benjamin, Rector.

Church of the Holy Sepulchre, East 74th St. near Fourth Avenue. Rev. J. T. Smith, Rector.

Church of Santiago, 30 West 22d St.

Christ, Fifth Avenue cor. East 35th St. Rev. F. C. Ewer, Rector; Rev. T. McKee Brown, Assistant.

Du St. Esprit, 30 West 22d St. Rev. A. Verren, Rector.

Emmanuel Chapel, West 68th St. near Broadway. Rev. B. F. Miller, Rector.

Epiphany, 130 Stanton St. Rev. B. B. Leacock, Rector.

Good Shepherd, East 54th St. near Second Avenue.

Grace, 800 Broadway. Rev. Henry C. Potter, Rector.

Grace Chapel, 132 East 14th St. Rev. J. W. Cramer, Rector.

Heavenly Rest, Fifth Avenue near East 45th St. Rev. R. S. Howland, Rector; Rev. Thos. K. Conrad, Assistant.

Holy Apostles, Ninth Avenue cor. West 28th St. Rev. J. P. Lundy, Rector.

Holy Communion, Sixth Avenue cor. West 20th St. Rev. F. E. Lawrence, Rector.

Holy Martyrs, 39 Forsyth St. Rev. J. Millett, Rector.

Holy Trinity, Fifth Avenue cor. West 125th St. Rev. W. N. McVickar, Rector.

Holy Trinity, Madison Avenue cor. East 42d St. Rev. S. H. Tyng, jr., Rector.

Incarnation, Madison Avenue cor. East 35th St. Rev. H. E. Montgomery, Rector.

Intercession, West 154th St. cor. Tenth Avenue. Rev. J. H. Smith, Rector.

Madison Street Mission, 256 Madison St. Rev. J. N. McJilton, Minister.

Memorial Church of the Rev. H. Anthon, 139 West 48th St. Rev. R. H. Newton, Rector; Rev. W. B. T. Smith, Assistant.

Nativity, 70 Avenue C. Rev. Caleb Clapp, Rector.

Our Saviour, foot Pike St. Rev. Robt. W. Lewis, Minister.

Reconciliation, 242 East 31st St. Rev. N. L. Briggs, Rector.

Redeemer, Fourth Avenue cor. East 82d Street. Rev. J. W. Shackelford, Rector.

Redemption, Fifth Avenue cor. West 14th. Rev. U. Scott, Rector.

Reformation, 228 East 50th St. Rev. Abbott Brown, Rector.

Resurrection, Madison Avenue cor. East 47th St. Rev. E. O. Flagg, Rector.

Rutgers Street Mission, 54 Rutgers St. Rev. J. N. McJilton, Rector.

St. Alban's, Lexington Avenue cor. East 47th St.   Rev. C. W. Morrill, Rector.

St. Ambrose, 117 Thompson St.   Rev. F. Sill, Rector.

St. Andrew's, East 127th St. near Fourth Avenue.   Rev. G. B. Draper, Rector.

St. Ann's, 7 West 18th St.   Rev. Thos. Gallaudet, Rector; Rev. S. F. Holmes and Rev. H. H. Cole, Assistants.

St. Barnabas Chapel, 306 Mulberry St.   Rev. A. H. Warner, Minister.

St. Bartholomew's, Lafayette Place cor. Great Jones St.   Rev. S. Cook, Rector; Rev. H. Wellman, Assistant Minister.

St. Clement's, 108 Amity St.   Rev. T. A. Eaton, Rector.

St. George's, Rutherford Place cor. East 16th St.   Rev. Stephen H. Tyng, Rector; Rev. Morris A. Tyng, Assistant.

St. George's German Chapel, 420 East 14th St.

St. James, East 72d St. near Third Avenue.   Rev. C. B. Smith, Rector.

St. John Baptist, 261 Lexington Avenue.   Rev. C. R. Duffie, Rector.

St. John Evangelist, 222 West 11th St.   Rev. R. G. Quennell, Rector.

St. John's, 46 Varick St.   Rev. S. H. Weston, Rector.

St. Luke's, 483 Hudson St.   Rev. Isaac H. Tuttle, Rector.

St. Mark's, Stuyvesant St. near Second Avenue.

St. Mary's West 128th St. near Tenth Avenue.   Rev. C. C. Adams, Rector.

St. Mathias, 210 West 42d St.   Rev. N. E. Cornwall, Rector.

St. Michael's, Broadway cor. West 99th St.   Rev. T. McPeters, Rector.

St. Paul's, Broadway cor. Vesey St. Rev. B. J. Haight, Minister.

St. Paul's, East 84th St. near Fourth Avenue.

St. Peter's, 342 West 20th St.   Rev. A. B. Beach, Rector.

St. Phillip's (colored), 305 Mulberry St.

St. Stephen's, 20 East 29th St.   Rev. J. H. Price, Rector.

St. Thomas', Fifth Avenue cor. West 53d St.   Rev. W. F. Morgan, Rector; Rev. J. B. Morgan, Assistant.

St. Timothy's, West 57th St. near Eighth Avenue.   Rev. G. J. Geer, Rector.

Transfiguration, East 29th St. near Fifth Avenue.   Rev. G. H. Houghton, Rector.

Trinity, Broadway cor. Rector St., and the Chapels of St. Paul's, St. John's, and Trinity Chapel. Rev. Morgan Dix, Rector; Rev. F. Vinton and Rev. F. Ogilby, Assistant Ministers.

Trinity Chapel, 15 West 25th St.   Rev. E. Y. Higbee, Rev. C. E. Swope, and Rev. C. T. Olmstead, Assistant Ministers.

Union (colored), Second Avenue, near East 84th St.

Zion, Madison Avenue cor. East 38th St.

REFORMED (Dutch).

Bloomingdale, West 71st St. near Ninth Avenue. Rev. E. Vanaken, Minister.

Collegiate, Lafayette Place, cor. East 4th St.; North Dutch, William St. cor. Fulton; Fifth Avenue, cor. West 29th St.; Chapel, West 48th St. near 5th Avenue. Rev. Thomas Dewitt, Rev. T. E. Vermilye, Rev. T. W. Chambers, Rev. James M. Ludlow, Ministers.

Collegiate Church Chapel, Seventh Avenue cor. West 54th St. Rev. W. H. Clark, Minister.

Fourth German Mission, 1287 Broadway. Rev. J. H. Oerter, Minister.

German Evangelical Mission, 141 East Houston St. Rev. J. W. Geyer, Minister.

German Ref. Prot., 129 Norfolk St. Rev. H. A. Freidel, Minister.

Harlem, Third Avenue corner East 121st St. Rev. G. H. Mundeville, Minister.

Knox Memorial, Ninth Avenue near West 39th St.

Manhattan, 71 Avenue B.

North Dutch Church Mission, Rev. J. L. McNair, Missionary. William St. cor Fulton St.

North West, Madison Avenue corner East 57th St. Rev. H. D. Ganse, Minister.

Prospect Hill, East 85th St. near Second Avenue. Rev. D. McL. Quackenbush, Minister.

St. Paul's, 40th St. near Sixth Avenue. Rev. A. R. Thompson, Minister.

South, Fifth Avenue corner West 21st St. Rev. E. P. Rogers, Minister.

Thirty-Fourth Street, 307 West 34th St. Rev. Isaac Riley, Minister.

Twenty-Ninth Street Mission Chapel, 160 West 29th St. Rev. J. H. Bertholf, Minister.

Union, 25 Sixth Avenue. Rev. J. L. Danner, Minister.

Washington Square, Washington Square East, corner Washington Place. Rev. M. S. Hutton, Minister.

ROMAN CATHOLIC.

St. Patrick's Cathedral, Mott St. cor. Prince. Most Rev. John McCloskey, Archbishop; Very Rev. William Starrs, Vicar-general; Rev. T. S. Preston, Chancellor; Rev. F. McNeirny, Secretary. Rev. P. F. McSweeny, Rev. J. H. McGean, and Rev. J. Kearney, Assistant Pastors.

Annunciation, B. V. M., West 131st St. near Broadway. Rev. John Breen, Pastor.

Assumption, 427 West 49th Street. Rev. B. Stroehle, Pastor.

Epiphany, 373 Second Avenue. Rev. R. L. Burtsell, Pastor.

Holy Cross, 335 West 42d St. Rev. P. McCarthy, Pastor.

Holy Innocents, 126 West 37th St. Rev. John Larkin, Pastor.

Holy Name of Jesus, Broadway near West 97th St. Rev. R. Brennan, Pastor.

Immaculate Conception, 505 East 14th St. Rev. W. P. Morrogh, Pastor.

Most Holy Redeemer, 165 Third St. Rev. M. Leimgruber, Pastor.

Nativity, 46 Second Avenue. Rev. William Everett, Pastor.

Our Lady of Sorrows, 105 Pitt St. Rev. C. Krauthahn, Pastor.

St. Alphonsus, 10 Thompson St.

St. Andrew's, Duane St. cor. City Hall Place. Rev. M. Curran, Pastor.

St. Ann's, East 12th St. between Third and Fourth avenues. Rev. T. S. Preston, Pastor.

St. Anthony, 149 Sullivan Street. Rev. C. da Nazzano, Pastor.

St. Boniface, Second Avenue corner East 47th St. Rev. M. Nicot, Pastor.

St. Bridget's, Avenue B, corner Eighth St. Rev. Thomas J. Mooney, Pastor.

St. Columba's, 339 West 25th St. Rev. M. McAleer, Pastor.

St. Francis, 139 West 31st St. Rev. Eugene Dikovich, Pastor.

St. Francis Xavier, 36 West 16th St. Rev. Victor Beaudevin, Pastor.

St. Gabriel's, East 37th St. near Second Avenue. Rev. W. H. Clowry, Pastor.

St. James, 32 James St. Rev. F. H. Farrelly, Pastor.

St John Baptist, 209 West 30th St. Rev. B. Frey, Pastor.

St. John Evangelist, East 50th St. near Fourth Avenue. Rev. James McMahon, Pastor.

St. Joseph's, Sixth Avenue cor. West Washington Place. Rev. Thomas Farrell, Pastor.

St. Joseph's (German), West 125th St. near Ninth Avenue. Rev. Anthony Kesseler, Pastor.

St. Lawrence, East 84th St. near Fourth Avenue. Rev. William Moylan, Pastor.

St. Mary's, 438 Grand St. Rev. E. J. O'Reilly, Pastor.

St. Michael's, 407 West 31st St. Rev. A. J. Donnelly, Pastor.

St. Nicholas, 125 Second St. Rev. F. Krebes, Pastor.

St Paul's, West 59th St. near Ninth Avenue. Rev. J. T. Hecker, Pastor.

St. Paul's, East 117th St. near Fourth Avenue. Rev. Eugene Maguire, Pastor.

St. Peter's, Barclay St. corner Church. Rev. William Quinn, Pastor.

St. Rose, 42 Cannon St. Rev. M. McKenna, Pastor.
St. Stephen's, 149 East 28th St. Rev. Dr. E. McGlynn,
Pastor.
St. Teresa, Rutgers St. cor. Henry. Rev. James Boyce, Pastor.
St. Vincent Ferrer, Lexington Avenue, corner East 66th St.
Rev. M. D. Lilly, Pastor.
St. Vincent de Paul, 127 West 23d St. Rev. Annet Lafont,
Pastor.
Transfiguration, Mott St. cor. Park St. Rev. Thomas Treanor,
Pastor.

UNITARIAN.

All Souls, Fourth Avenue cor. East 20th St. Rev. H. W.
Bellows, Minister.
Messiah, East 34th St. cor. Park Avenue. Rev. George H.
Hepworth, Minister.
Third, Sixth Avenue near West 41st St. Rev. O. B. Frothing-
ham, Minister.

UNIVERSALIST.

Fifth, Stuyvesant, corner East 9th St.
Third, 214 Bleecker St. Rev. E. C. Sweetser, Minister.
Fourth, Fifth Avenue cor. West 45th St. Rev. E. H. Chapin,
Minister.
Harlem Mission, East 129th St. cor. Third Avenue.
Mission, East 54th St. near Third Avenue. Rev. C. Fluhrer,
Minister.
Our Saviour, 65 West 35th St. Rev. James M. Pullman, Minister.

MISCELLANEOUS.

Catholic Apostolic, 128 West 16th St. D. M. Fackler, Angel in
charge.
Centre Street Mission, 119 Elm St.
Christian Church, 24 West 28th St. E. Parmly and George A.
Merwin, Elders; C. C. Foote, Minister.
Christian Israelites, 108 First St. Frederick Thomas, Minister.
Church of the Strangers, Mercer Street near Waverly Place.
Charles F. Deems, Minister.
Evangelical, rear 138 West 24th St. I. E. Knerr, Minister.
First Methodist Protestant, 87 Attorney St.
Free Evangelical Chapel, East 110th St. near Third Avenue.
German Evangelical Reformed, 97 Suffolk St. J. F. Busche,
Minister.
Mariner's, Madison St. cor. Catherine. E. D. Murphy.
Messiah's, 7 Seventh Avenue.
Mission, 27 Greenwich St. George Hatt, Minister.

Seventh Day Baptist, Second Avenue cor. East 11th St.

Swedenborgian First New Church Society, 114 East 35th St. Chauney Giles, Minister.

True Dutch Reformed, Perry St. cor. West 4th St. A. Vanhoughten, Minister.

United Brethren (Moravian), Lexington Avenue cor. East 30th St.

Welsh, Methodist Calvinistic, 225 East 13th St.

BANKS.

NATIONAL.

American, 542 Broadway: Capital, $500,000; Joseph Pool, President; A. B. Proal, Cashier.

American Exchange, 128 Broadway: Capital, $5,000,000; George S. Coe, President; E. Willson, Cashier.

Atlantic, 142 Broadway: Capital, $300,000; J. E. Southworth, President; T. L. Taintor, Cashier.

Bank of Commerce, Nassau cor. Cedar Street: Capital $10,000,000; Robert Lenox Kennedy, President; Henry F. Vail, Cashier.

Bank of New York, 48 Wall Street: Capital, $3,000,000; C. P. Leverich, President; W. B. Meeker, Cashier.

Bank of the Commonwealth, 15 Nassau Street: Capital, $750,000; Edward Haight, President; George Ellis, Cashier.

Bank of the State of New York, 33 William Street: Capital, $2,000,000; G. W. Duer, President; J. R. Kearney, Cashier.

Bank of the Republic, Wall St. cor. Broadway: Capital, $2,000,000; R. H. Lowry, President; H. W. Ford, Cashier.

Bowery, 62 Bowery: Capital, $250,000; H. P. Degraaf, President; R. Hamilton, Cashier.

Broadway, 237 Broadway: Capital, $1,000,000; F. A. Palmer, President; John L. Everett, Cashier.

Butchers' and Drovers', 124 Bowery: Capital, $800,000; R. P. Perin, President; G. G. Brinckerhoff, Cashier.

Central, 320 Broadway: Capital $3,000,000; W. A. Wheelock, President; C. F. Coles, Cashier.

Chatham, 184 Broadway: Capital, $450,000; Nathaniel Hayden, President; O. H. Schreener, Cashier.

Chemical, 270 Broadway: Capital, $300,000; John Q. Jones, President; George G. Williams, Cashier.

Citizens, 381 Broadway: Capital, $400,000; S. R. Comstock, President; W. H. Oakley, Cashier.

City, 52 Wall Street: Capital, $1,000,000; Moses Taylor, President; B. Cartwright, Cashier.

Continental, 7 Nassau Street: Capital, $2,000,000; Thompson J. S. Flint, President; C. F. Timpson, Cashier.

East River, 682 Broadway: Capital, $350,000; Charles Jenkins, President; Z. E. Newell, Cashier.

Eighth, 650 Broadway: Capital, $250,000; Union Adams, President; Charles Hudson, Cashier.

Fifth, 366 Third Avenue: Richard Kelly, President; A. Thompson, Cashier.

First, 140 Broadway: Capital, $500,000; C. S. Thompson, President; G. F. Baker, Cashier.

Fourth, Nassau cor. Pine Street: Capital, $5,000,000. P. Calhoun, President; Joseph Stewart, Vice President; R. Seaman, Cashier; A. Lane, Assistant Cashier.

Fulton, Fulton cor. Pearl Street : Capital $600,000. Thomas Monahan, President; R. H. Haydock, Cashier.

Gallatin, 36 Wall Street: Capital $1,500,000. F. D. Tappen, President; A. H. Stevens, Cashier.

Grocers, 59 Barclay Street, Capital, $300,000, E. Rowe, President; Samuel B. White, Cashier.

Hanover, 33 Wall Street: Capital, $1,000,000 ; W. H. Johnson, President: J. T. Banker, Cashier.

Importers' and Traders', 247 Broadway ; Capital, $1,500,000, James Buell, President: E. H. Perkins, Jr., Cashier.

Irving, Greenwich cor. Warren Street: Capital, $500,000; John Castree, President; John L. Jewett, Jr., Cashier.

Leather Manufacturers, 29 Wall Street: Capital, $600,000; William A. Macy, President; N. F. Palmer, Cashier.

Marine, 90 Wall Street: Capital, $400.000; J. D. Fish, President; J. W. Elwell, Vice President; J. Delamater, Cashier.

Market, Pearl cor. of Beekman Street: Capital, $1,000,000; R. Bayles, President; A. Gillert, Cashier.

Mechanics, 38 Wall Street: Capital, $2,000,000; Shepherd Knapp, President, W. H. Cox, Cashier.

Mechanics Banking Association, 38 Wall Street: Capital. $500,-000: Mason Thomson, President; F. Chandler, Cashier.

Mechanics and Traders, 153 Bowery: Capital, $600,000; E. D. Brown, President; G. H. Youle, Cashier.

Mercantile, 191 Bowery: Capital, $1,000,000; E. J. Blake, President; A. Amerman, Cashier.

Merchants, 42 Wall Street: Capital, $3,000,000; Jacob D. Vermilye, President; Robt. McCartee, Cashier.

Merchants Exchange, 257 Broadway: Capital, $1,235,000; Wm. A. Thomson, President; A. S. Apger, Cashier.

Metropolitan, 108 Broadway: Capital, $4,000,000; John E. Williams, President; Geo. I. Seney, Cashier.

National Currency, Wall St. cor. Broadway; F. F. Thompson. President; J. L. Morford, Cashier.

New York County, 81 Eighth Avenue: Capital, $200,000; Francis Leland, President; Geo. H. Wyckoff, Cashier.

New York National Exchange, Chambers St. cor. College Place: Capital, $500,000; Selah Vanduzer, President; D. B. Halstead, Cashier.

Ninth, 407 and 409 Broadway: Capital, $1,000,000; Thos. A. Vyse, Jr., President; John T. Hill, Cashier.

Ocean, Greenwich cor. Fulton Street: Capital. $1,000,000; D. R. Martin, President; C. S. Stevenson, Cashier.

Park, 214 and 216 Broadway: Capital, $2,000,000; W. K. Kitchen, President; J. L. Worth, Cashier.

Phenix, 45 Wall Street: Capital, $1,800,000; P. M. Byrson, President; J. Parker, Cashier.

St. Nicholas, 7 Wall Street: Capital, $1,000,000; J. L. Smith, President; Archibald Parkhurst, Cashier.

Second, Fifth Avenue cor. West Twenty-Third Street: Capital, 300,000; Amos H. Trowbridge, President; O. D. Roberts, Cashier.

Seventh Ward, 234 Pearl Street: Capital, $500,000; A. S. Fraser, President; G. Montague, Cashier.

Shoe and Leather, 271 Broadway: Capital, $1,500,000; A. V. Stout, President; J. M. Crane, Cashier.

Sixth, West Thirty-Fifth Street cor. Broadway: Capital, $200,-000; Cassius Darling, President; Geo. G. Haven, Vice President; A. E. Colson, Cashier.

Tenth, 348 Broadway: Capital, $1,000,000; Wm. M. Bliss, President; Bernard Smyth, Vice President; Walter B. Palmer, Cashier.

Third, 29 Pine Street: Capital, $1,000,000; J. F. D. Lanier, President; James Winslow, Vice President; C. N. Jordan, Cashier.

Tradesmen's, 291 Broadway: Capital, $1,000,000; Rich. Berry, President; A. Halsey, Cashier.

Union, 34 Wall Street: Capital $1,500,000; A. M. White, President; James M. Lewis, Cashier.

Union Square, 23 Union Place: Capital. $200,000; Henry Beeckman, President; M. T. Brundage, Cashier.

STATE.

Bank of America, 46 Wall Street: Capital, $3,000,000; James Punnett, President; Wm. L. Jenkins, Cashier.

Bank of North America, 44 Wall Street: Capital, $1,000,000; John J. Donaldson, President; J. A. Beardsley, Cashier.

Bull's Head, 340 Third Avenue: Capital, $200,000; Richard Williamson, President; George F. Willett, Cashier.

Corn Exchange, 13 William Street: Capital, $1,000,000; E. W. Dunham, President; W. A. Falls, Cashier.

Eleventh Ward, Avenue D, cor. East Tenth Street: Capital $200,000; John Englis, President; C. E. Brown, Cashier.

Germania, 185 Bowery: Capital, $200,000; C. Schwarzwaelder, President; John W. Hesse, Cashier.

Greenwich, 402 Hudson Street: Capital, $200,000; B. F. Wheelwright, President; Wm. Hawes, Cashier.

Harlem, 2279 Third Avenue: Capital, $500,000; Adison Smith, President; Isaac Anderson, Cashier.

Manhattan, 40 Wall Street: Capital, $2,050,000; J. M. Morrison, President; J. S. Harberger, Cashier.

Manufacturer's and Builder's, 916 Third Avenue: Capital, $100,000; John Davidson, President; C. A. Waterbury, Cashier.

Manufacturer's and Merchant's, 561 Broadway: Capital, $500,-000; A. Masterton, President; T. D. Warren, Cashier.

Mutual, 750 Broadway: Capital, $200,000; Wm. L. Conklin, President; Wm. S. Carman, Cashier.

Nassau, Nassau cor. Beekman Street: Capital, $1,000,000; F. M. Harris, President; W. H. Rogers, Cashier.

N. Y. Gold Exchange, 68 Broadway: Capital, $500,000; Jacob Russell, President; H. C. Rogers, Cashier.

North River, 187 Greenwich Street: Capital, $400,000; L. Apgar, President; A. B. Hays, Cashier.

Oriental, 122 Bowery: Capital $300,000; W. A. Hall, President; H. T. Chapman, Jr., Cashier.

Pacific, 470 Broadway: Capital, $422,700; Jacob Campbell, President; Robert Buck, Cashier.

People's, 395 Canal Street: Capital, $412,500; C. F. Hunter, President; I. N. Zabriskie, Cashier.

Stuyvesant, 744 Broadway: Capital, $200,000; Davis Collamore, President; John Vanorden, Cashier.

West Side, Eighth Avenue cor. West Thirty-Fourth Street: Capital $200,000; George Moore, President; John W. B. Dobler, Cashier.

PLACES OF AMUSEMENT.

Niblo's Garden, Metropolitan Hotel.

Fifth Avenue Theatre, Twenty-Fourth St. near Broadway.

Olympic Theatre, Broadway, between Bleecker and Houston Sts

Steinway Hall, Fourteenth St. between Irving Place and Fourth Avenue.

Wallack's Theatre, Broadway, near Thirteenth St.
Theatre Comique, 514 Broadway.
Booth's Theatre, cor. of Twenty-Third St. and Sixth Avenue.
Lina Edwin's Theatre, Broadway, opposite New York Hotel.
Bowery Theatre, 46 Bowery.
New York Circus, Fourteenth St. between Third and Fourth
    Avenues.
Stadt Theatre, 37 and 39 Bowery.
Bryant's Opera House, Twenty-Third St. between Sixth and
    Seventh Avenues.
Grand Opera House, cor. of Twenty-Third St. and Eighth
    Avenues.
Globe Theatre, 728 Broadway.
Wood's Museum, Broadway, near Thirteenth St.
San Francisco Minstrels, 585 Broadway.
Academy of Music, Fourteenth St. cor. of Irving Place.
Fourteenth Street Theatre, Fourteenth St. near Sixth Avenue.

RAILROAD DEPOTS.

Hudson River, Thirteenth St. and Tenth Avenue.
New York and Harlem, Fourth Avenue and 26th St.
New York and New Haven, Twenty-Seventh St. and Fourth
    Avenue.
New York and Erie, foot of Chambers and West 23d streets.
New Jersey, foot of Desbrosses St.
New Jersey Central, foot of Liberty St.
Newark and New York, foot of Liberty St.
Morris and Essex, foot of Barclay and Christopher Sts.
Northern, of New Jersey, foot of Chambers St. (Pavonia
    Ferry).
New Jersey Southern. Pier 28, North River.
South Side of Long Island, leaves Roosevelt and Grand St.
    Ferries.
Long Island, foot of James Slip and Thirty-Fourth St., East
    River.
Flushing and North Side, same as Long Island.
Hackensack and New York, foot of Chambers Street.
Staten Island, foot Whitehall St.
Camden and Amboy, Pier 1, North River.
Brooklyn Central and Jamaica.

LEADING HOTELS.

Fifth Avenue Hotel, Broadway and 23d St.
St. Nicholas Hotel, No. 515 Broadway.
Metropolitan Hotel, No. 580 Broadway.
New York Hotel, No. 781 Broadway.
Clarendon Hotel, No. 60 Union Place.
Grand Central Hotel, Broadway opp. Bond St.
Spingler House, No. 5 Union Square.
Union Place Hotel, No. 58 East 14th St.
Gramercy Park House, Gramercy Park.
Wadsworth House, No. 63 Fifth Avenue.
Lenox House, No. 72 Fifth Avenue.
Maltby House, No. 23 Great Jones St.
Merchant's Hotel, No. 41 Courtlandt St.
Earle's Hotel, No. 241 Canal St.
Brandreth House, Broadway and Canal St.
Western Hotel, No. 11 Courtlandt St.

The following Hotels are conducted on the European Plan.

Everett House, 17th St. cor. Fourth Avenue.
St. James Hotel, No. 1135 Broadway.
Hoffman House, No. 1111 Broadway.
Albemarle Hotel, No. 1101 Broadway.
St. Denis Hotel, No. 797 Broadway.
Brevoort House, No. 11 Fifth Avenue.
Westminster Hotel, No. 119 East 16th St.
Coleman House No. 1169 Broadway.
Grand Hotel, No. 1230 Broadway.
Astor House, Broadway and Vesey St.
St. Cloud Hotel, Broadway and 42d St.
Prescott House, No. 531 Broadway.
National Hotel, No. 5 Courtlandt St.
Courtlandt St. Hotel, No. 28 Courtlandt St.
Stevens House, No. 25 Broadway.
French's Hotel, No. 1 Chatham St.
Sweeny's Hotel, No. 68 Chatham St.
Park Hotel, No. 12 Beekman St.
Commercial Hotel, No. 17 Park Row.

LIBRARIES.

Apprentices', 472 Broadway. William **Vannorden**, Librarian. Open from 8 A. M. to 9 P. M. Apprentices and females employed by mechanics and tradesmen in their business, receive books gratis; journeymen and others upon the payment of two dollars per annum.

Astor, Lafayette Place near Astor Place. William B. Astor, President; F. Schroeder, Librarian. Open daily except Sundays and holidays, from 9.30 A. M. to 5 P. M. Free.

City, 12 City Hall. Open daily from 10 A. M. to 4 P. M. James Barclay, Librarian. Free to all persons.

Cooper Union, Seventh St. cor. Fourth Avenue. E. M. Schroeder, Librarian. Open from 8 A. M. to 10 P. M.

Harlem, 2238 Third Av. D. P. Ingraham, President. Terms, $2 per annum. Open from 2 to 7 P. M.

Library of the American Institute, Cooper Union. John W. Chambers, Librarian. Open daily from 9 A. M. to 9 P. M. Terms of membership of the (Institute and) Library, $5 initiation fee, and $3 per annum.

Mercantile Library Association, Astor Place. A. M. Palmer, Librarian. Open from 8 A. M. to 9 P. M.; Down town office, 76 Cedar St. Terms of membership : For clerks, $1 initiation fee, and $3 per annum; merchants and others, $5 annually. Reading room open from 8 A. M. to 10 P. M.

Mott Memorial Free Medical, 64 Madison Avenue. A. B. Mott, Director. Open daily from 11 A. M. to 9 P. M.

New York Historical Society, Second Avenue cor. East 11th Street. George H. Moore, Librarian. Open, from October to April, from 9 A. M. to 9 P. M.; from April to October, from 9 A. M. to 6 P. M.

New York Law Institute, 41 Chambers St. Open daily (except Sundays) from 9 A. M. to 5 P. M. A. J. Vanderpoel, Librarian. Terms of membership, $150, subject to assessments.

New York Society, 67 University Place. Frederick Depeyster. President; W. S. Butler, Librarian. Open from 8 A. M. until 6 P. M.; Reading room from 8 A. M. to 10 P. M. Terms of membership, $25 for a transferable right, subject to an annual payment of $10. Temporary subscription ,$15 per annum ; $8 for six months; $5 for three months. Free shares, $150.

Printers', 3 Chambers Street. John Craw, Librarian. Open last Saturday evening in each month. The Library contains over 4,000 volumes. There is no charge made, except where persons take books from the Library, for which privilege $1 a year is charged.

Washington Heights, Tenth Avenue near West 160th Street.
John McMullen, Secretary ; John L. Tonnellie, Treasurer.

Woman's, 38 Bleecker Street. John D. Wolfe, President ;
Moses S. Beach, Treasurer; Mrs. M. W. Ferrer, Superin-
tendent. Open daily from 9 A. M. to 4 P. M. Terms of
membership, $1.50 per annum.

Young Men's Christian Association, East 23d Street cor.
Fourth Avenue; Third Avenue cor East 122d St., 285 Hudson St., 473 Grand St., and 97 Wooster St. R. B. Pool,
Librarian. Open daily from 8 A. M. to 10 P. M., and Sundays from 1 to 9.30 P. M. Terms of membership: Persons
under forty years of age, $2 per annum; over forty, $5 per
annum; life membership, $100.

——◇——

FERRIES.

Astoria, foot of East 92d St.
Brooklyn, Catherine Slip to Main St.
Brooklyn, foot Fulton Street to Fulton St.
Brooklyn, foot Jackson Street to Hudson Avenue.
Brooklyn, foot Wall Street to Montague St.
Brooklyn, foot Whitehall Street to Atlantic St.
Brooklyn, foot New Chambers Street to Bridge St.
Brooklyn, (E. D.) foot Roosevelt Street to South 7th St.
Brooklyn, (E. D.) foot East Houston Street to Grand St.
Brooklyn, (E. D.) foot Grand St. to Grand St. and South 7th St.
Bull's Ferry and Fort Lee, Pier 43 North River.
Communipaw, foot Liberty St.
Greenpoint, foot East 10th Street and foot East 23d St.
Hamilton Avenue, foot Whitehall Street to Atlantic Dock.
Hoboken, foot Barclay St.
Hoboken, foot Christopher St.
Hunter's Point, foot East 34th Street to Ferry St.
Hunter's Point, James Slip to Ferry St.
Jersey City, foot Courtlandt Street to Montgomery St.
Jersey City, foot Desbrosses Street to Exchange Place.
Jersey City, foot 23d Street to Long Dock.
Mott Haven, Pier 24 East River.
Pavonia, foot Chambers Street, North River, to Long Dock.
Staten Island (Tomkinsville, Stapleton, and Vanderbilt's Land-
ing), foot Whitehall St.
Staten Island (New Brighton, Castleton, Port Richmond, and
Elm Park), Pier 19 North River.
Wehawken, foot West 42d St.

GOVERNOR'S ISLAND.

The steamer Josephine Hoey will leave as follows: —

Pier 1, East River, 7.30, 9, 10, 10.45, and 11.30 A. M.; 12.30, 2, 3.30, 4.30, 5.45, and 6.50 P. M.

RETURNING:

Leave Governor's Island, 7.15, 8.30, 9.30, 10.30, and 11.15 A. M.; 12 M.; 1.30, 3, 4, 5.30, and 6.45 P. M.; and 7 P. M. for Brooklyn only.

— ● —

CEMETERIES.

Cemetery of the Evergreens, office 124 Bowery. Myrtle Avenue and Jamaica Plank Road. Five miles from Williamsburg ferries, thence by Broadway cars.

Greenwood, office 30 Broadway. Brooklyn, on Gowanus Heights. *Via* street cars from Fulton or South ferries.

Calvary, office 266 Mulberry St. Newton, L. I. Two miles from East 10th St. Ferry, or *via* Grand St. Ferry. Take Grand St. and Meeker Avenue cars.

Marble, office 65 Second St. Grounds, Second St. between First and Second Avenues. Take Second St. stages.

New York Bay, office 195 Broadway. Bergen Point Plank Road, two and a half miles from Jersey City Ferry. Take Plank Road cars.

Trinity Church, office 187 Fulton St. Between West 153d and West 155th St. and Tenth Avenue and the North River. Take Eighth Avenue cars.

Union, office 192 Rivington St. Wyckoff Avenue, Brooklyn. Three and a half miles from Division Avenue Ferry. Take Broadway cars, or, *via* Fulton Ferry, take Myrtle Avenue cars.

Woodlawn, office 56 East 26th St. Westchester County, seven miles from Harlem Bridge, on the line of the Harlem Railroad.

Lutheran, office 203 Broadway. Jamaica Turnpike Road, near Middle Village, L. I. Four miles from Grand St Ferry. Take Grand St. cars.

Machpelah, office 169 West 24th St. New Durham, Hudson Co., N. J. One mile from Wehawken Ferry.

Cypress Hills Cemetery, Jamaica Plank Road, East New York. About five miles from Fulton or South ferries, *via* street cars.

For further particulars regarding the Brooklyn Cemeteries, see Brooklyn.

BROOKLYN.

PROSPECT PARK.

THE natural inference from the fact that we have given so much space to Central Park and so little to Prospect Park, would be that the latter is scarce worthy of notice. Such a conclusion would, however, be far from just, and to the visitor to New York who condescends to be guided by our suggestions, we would say that, next to the former, there is no public work in New York or vicinity, so interesting as the latter. It occupies an irregular piece of ground about five hundred acres in extent, lying to the southeast of the city of Brooklyn. The principal entrance is at the intersection of Flatbush and Vanderbilt avenues, and the means of access from New York, are by the Fulton Ferry and street cars.

Near to the magnificent fountain by the main entrance is the bronze statue of Mr. Lincoln, erected at an expense of thirteen thousand dollars, by one dollar subscriptions from the people of Brooklyn.

Within the Park there is much less of artistic detail to be described than in the Central Park, and the effort seems to have been to supplement the rich natural features of the place by the production of magnificent general effects. In *natural* beauty of location and incident, the Prospect Park stands, and will remain, peerless among all the pleasure grounds of this country. A splendid growth of native forest trees, bold eminences commanding extensive views over sea and land; water-courses and lakes, just as nature made them, give a charm of freshness that no art can supply. These features have been developed by a lavish outlay of money, guided by a consummate skill and taste, so that as a result we have grand combinations of nature and art, so deftly managed that we cannot define the line where nature ceases and art begins.

Botanical gardens, zoölogical gardens, and a deer paddock are features yet to be realized; but already there are miles of broad drives, bridle-paths, and foot-walks, leading over and around all the beautiful and interesting localities; while music stands, arbors, romantic bridges, terraces, and skating ponds, are some of the appliances which the landscape gardener and the architect have availed of to perfect the purpose of the Park.

Brooklyn is proud of her Park, and the annual visitors, already counted by millions, testify the general appreciation of the privileges it affords; while the advance in the value of surrounding property, to say nothing of the more important influences upon the health and culture of the people, fully justifies the immense outlay it has involved.

THE PARADE GROUND.

Directly opposite the southern boundary of the Prospect Park is the Kings County Parade Ground, conceded to be the finest ground for the purpose in the United States. Being thoroughly under drained, the earth solid, as level as a floor, and the turf neatly cut, it affords the National Guard of Brooklyn unequaled facilities for military exercise and parade. It is frequently used for drill and review by the military of New York. The Coney Island cars run directly to, and the Flatbush cars very nearly to the Parade Ground, both from Fulton Ferry.

WASHINGTON PARK.

This, the oldest Park in Brooklyn, is the only one worthy of notice aside from the Prospect Park. It occupies a commanding eminence, the site of Fort Green of Revolutionary fame, and not only from historic interest, but also on account of the fine view and tasteful arrangement of the Park itself, is a popular resort. The play-grounds and bower shelters are extensive and beautiful, making it the rendezvous of all the children within convenient access to it. The Myrtle Avenue cars pass on the north, and the Green Avenue cars on the south side of this Park.

GREENWOOD CEMETERY.

This most beautiful resting-place of the dead is situated in South Brooklyn, on the heights overlooking Gowanus Bay, the main entrance being on Fifth Avenue, directly opposite the termination of Twenty-Fifth Street, and may be reached from New York by Fulton or South ferries, and thence by street cars. The natural beauties of the place are of a high order, and these with the artistic effects of the ornamented vaults, the embellishments of the inclosed lots, and the varied and beautiful monuments, combine to reward in abundant measure the time and trouble expended in the visit.

Worthy of special note as the more prominent incidents of Greenwood, are the main entrance gate with its sculptures of the entombment and resurrection of the Saviour; the bringing to life of the Widow's Son, and the raising of Lazarus; surmounted by the figures of Faith, Hope, Memory, and Love: the bronze statue of DeWitt Clinton, the monument to Miss Charlotte Canda, and the Pilot's and Fireman's monuments. Greenwood Cemetery in detail would require a book of itself, and would then fail to convey a correct idea; to appreciate and enjoy this lovely place the visit should be made with leisure, and a ramble on foot, if time allows, will reveal more of the beauties and afford greater gratification than a carriage drive through the grounds.

CYPRESS HILLS CEMETERY

Is near East New York, about five miles from the ferries. The most convenient route from New York is *via* South Ferry and East New York cars.

This cemetery is chiefly remarkable from its commanding position, which affords so extensive and beautiful views. There have been 35,000 bodies transferred from the city burying grounds; beside them are many veterans of the War of 1812, and 3,500 Union soldiers, victims of the late war, also interred here. The Masonic Fraternity, Odd Fellows, and Sons of Temperance, all have burial plots in this Cemetery.

CEMETERY OF THE HOLY CROSS.

This is a small cemetery devoted entirely to the use of Roman Catholics; it has many beautiful monuments, and is under the control of the Bishop of Brooklyn. From its location in Flatbush, it is often designated as the Flatbush Cemetery.

THE MERCANTILE LIBRARY BUILDING.

This building on Montague near Court Street, is a peculiar and beautiful structure of admirable design and perfect adaptation to its uses.

The library is large and rapidly increasing.

This is an institution that well deserves a visit from those interested in the subject of libraries for the people.

THE ART ASSOCIATION BUILDING,

Which is now in course of erection on Montague Street, near Clinton, will be a fine Gothic structure, at once an ornament to the city and a credit to the association.

THE ACADEMY OF MUSIC

Is perhaps not legitimately an object of mention in a book of this character, as there are many similar structures in other cities quite its equals or superiors, but this building stands in such peculiar relations to the Brooklyn community as a rallying point in social amusements, the drama, art, charity, and politics, that its status is different from similar buildings elsewhere.

It is on Montague Street, near Court, a gloomy looking pile, but within, quite pleasant and comfortable.

KING'S COUNTY COURT-HOUSE,

On Joralemon Street facing Fulton Street, is a handsome building of Westchester marble, built in the Corinthian style in 1861, at a cost of $550,000.

It has a front of ninety feet, with a depth of one hundred and forty feet, and is the most imposing public building in Brooklyn.

THE CITY HALL

Stands in a small triangular park, bounded by Court, Fulton, and Joralemon streets.

It is a commanding white marble building of fine proportions, and sufficiently spacious to accommodate all the city officers.

THE ATLANTIC DOCK.

The warehouse business of the city of Brooklyn is a most important interest, and well worthy of examination by the curious. The most important structure connected with this trade is the Atlantic Dock in South Brooklyn, on the water front opposite Governor's Island, where twenty acres of warehouses inclose a basin of forty acres of water, of sufficient depth to allow the largest ships to discharge cargo at their very doors. The accommodations here are such, that an immense business in grain, sugar, molasses, etc., is carried on with ease and facility.

THE NAVY YARD.

The naval station at Brooklyn is the most important in the country, and from the extent of the grounds occupied, the number of war vessels constantly here, and the variety of work always going forward, is a most interesting place to visit. The naval museum, marine barracks, and the immense dry dock that cost $2,000,000, and will accomodate a ship 300 feet long, are all points of interest. The Navy Yard is easily reached from New York by the Fulton Ferry and Street cars.

EAST RIVER BRIDGE.

This stupendous work, it is estimated, will cost $8,000,000, and if carried out according to present plans, will be a mile and a quarter long, and of a sufficient height to allow the passage of the largest vessels.

Work upon it is now progressing at a point near Fulton Ferry, but the probable date of its completion is a mere matter of speculation.

RIDGEWOOD RESERVOIR.

The city of Brooklyn is supplied with an abundance of pure water, which is brought from Hempstead Pond and adjacent waters, by an aqueduct about twenty miles long. The main reservoir receiving the water supply, is located near East New York, and easily accessible by the street cars. It has a capacity of 160,000.000 gallons, but possesses no points of special interest. There is also a distributing reservoir of 20,000,000 gallons on Flatbush Avenue, adjacent to Prospect Park.

PLACES OF AMUSEMENT.

Academy of Music, Montague Street near Clinton St.

Hooley's Minstrels, Court Street cor. Remsen St.

Park Theatre, Fulton Street opposite the City Hall.

Organ Concerts are given at stated intervals in the Plymouth Church, Orange Street near Hicks St., and at the Tabernacle, Schermerhorn Street near Nevins St.

DIRECTIONS FOR MEASURING.

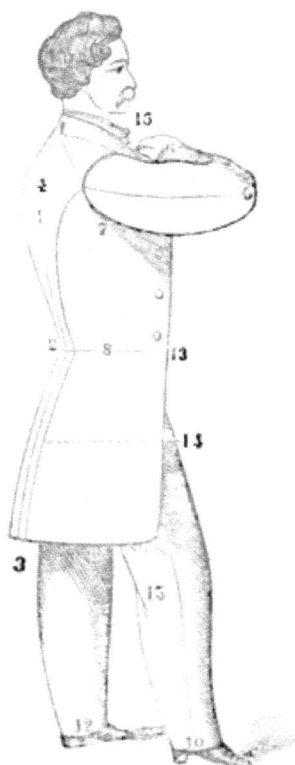

COAT.

Length, from 1 to 2 and 3.
Arm, 4 to 5 and 6.
Around the breast, under the coat, 7.
Around the waist, under the coat, 8.
Height, — feet — inches.
Weight, — lbs.

VEST.

Length, from 1 to 13, with last two coat measures.

PANTS.

Outside seam from top of waistband, 10.
Inside leg seam, from crotch, 12.
Around the waist, under the coat, 8.
Around the hips, under the coat, 14.

By the above system measures may be taken for Clothing to be supplied either ready made or to order. We give special attention to orders by this method, and are always happy to respond to requests for prices or other information.

DEVLIN & CO.

Box No. 2256, P. O.

NEW YORK.

AMERICAN
YOKE SHIRT

MODE OF MEASUREMENT.

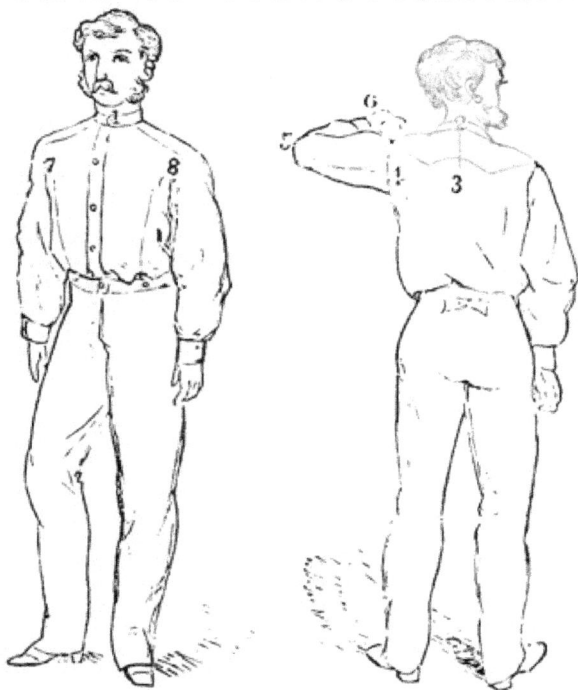

1. Size of neck at 1.
2. Length of shirt from 2.
3. Length of sleeve from 3 to 4 and 5 and 6.
4. Across breast from 7 to 8.
5. Around the breast.
6. Around the waist.
State whether with or without collar.

We are the sole Manufacturers of the above Shirt, which is without an equal for ease and elegance of fit. Orders filled from stock ready made, or to order if desired. Information by mail forwarded promptly when requested.

DEVLIN & CO.

Box No. 2256, P. O., New York.

www.ingramcontent.com/pod-product-compliance
Lightning Source LLC
Chambersburg PA
CBHW021633270326
41931CB00008B/1000